A dissuasive from popery. In a letter from the late Archbishop Tillotson, when Dean of Canterbury, to the Right Hon. Charles, then Earl, afterwards Duke of Shrewsbury.

John Tillotson

A dissuasive from popery. In a letter from the late Archbishop Tillotson, when Dean of Canterbury, to the Right Hon. Charles, then Earl, afterwards Duke of Shrewsbury.
Tillotson, John
ESTCID: T085272
Reproduction from Bodleian Library (Oxford)
Vertical chain-lines. Also issued as part of: 'Religious tracts, dispersed by the Society for Promoting Christian Knowledge', vol.XI, 1800.
London : printed for John Rivington, 1768.
24p. ; 12°

Eighteenth Century
Collections Online
Print Editions

Gale ECCO Print Editions

Relive history with *Eighteenth Century Collections Online*, now available in print for the independent historian and collector. This series includes the most significant English-language and foreign-language works printed in Great Britain during the eighteenth century, and is organized in seven different subject areas including literature and language; medicine, science, and technology; and religion and philosophy. The collection also includes thousands of important works from the Americas.

The eighteenth century has been called "The Age of Enlightenment." It was a period of rapid advance in print culture and publishing, in world exploration, and in the rapid growth of science and technology – all of which had a profound impact on the political and cultural landscape. At the end of the century the American Revolution, French Revolution and Industrial Revolution, perhaps three of the most significant events in modern history, set in motion developments that eventually dominated world political, economic, and social life.

In a groundbreaking effort, Gale initiated a revolution of its own: digitization of epic proportions to preserve these invaluable works in the largest online archive of its kind. Contributions from major world libraries constitute over 175,000 original printed works. Scanned images of the actual pages, rather than transcriptions, recreate the works *as they first appeared.*

Now for the first time, these high-quality digital scans of original works are available via print-on-demand, making them readily accessible to libraries, students, independent scholars, and readers of all ages.

For our initial release we have created seven robust collections to form one the world's most comprehensive catalogs of 18th century works.

Initial Gale ECCO Print Editions collections include:

History and Geography
Rich in titles on English life and social history, this collection spans the world as it was known to eighteenth-century historians and explorers. Titles include a wealth of travel accounts and diaries, histories of nations from throughout the world, and maps and charts of a world that was still being discovered. Students of the War of American Independence will find fascinating accounts from the British side of conflict.

Social Science
Delve into what it was like to live during the eighteenth century by reading the first-hand accounts of everyday people, including city dwellers and farmers, businessmen and bankers, artisans and merchants, artists and their patrons, politicians and their constituents. Original texts make the American, French, and Industrial revolutions vividly contemporary.

Medicine, Science and Technology
Medical theory and practice of the 1700s developed rapidly, as is evidenced by the extensive collection, which includes descriptions of diseases, their conditions, and treatments. Books on science and technology, agriculture, military technology, natural philosophy, even cookbooks, are all contained here.

Literature and Language
Western literary study flows out of eighteenth-century works by Alexander Pope, Daniel Defoe, Henry Fielding, Frances Burney, Denis Diderot, Johann Gottfried Herder, Johann Wolfgang von Goethe, and others. Experience the birth of the modern novel, or compare the development of language using dictionaries and grammar discourses.

Religion and Philosophy
The Age of Enlightenment profoundly enriched religious and philosophical understanding and continues to influence present-day thinking. Works collected here include masterpieces by David Hume, Immanuel Kant, and Jean-Jacques Rousseau, as well as religious sermons and moral debates on the issues of the day, such as the slave trade. The Age of Reason saw conflict between Protestantism and Catholicism transformed into one between faith and logic -- a debate that continues in the twenty-first century.

Law and Reference
This collection reveals the history of English common law and Empire law in a vastly changing world of British expansion. Dominating the legal field is the *Commentaries of the Law of England* by Sir William Blackstone, which first appeared in 1765. Reference works such as almanacs and catalogues continue to educate us by revealing the day-to-day workings of society.

Fine Arts
The eighteenth-century fascination with Greek and Roman antiquity followed the systematic excavation of the ruins at Pompeii and Herculaneum in southern Italy; and after 1750 a neoclassical style dominated all artistic fields. The titles here trace developments in mostly English-language works on painting, sculpture, architecture, music, theater, and other disciplines. Instructional works on musical instruments, catalogs of art objects, comic operas, and more are also included.

The BiblioLife Network

This project was made possible in part by the BiblioLife Network (BLN), a project aimed at addressing some of the huge challenges facing book preservationists around the world. The BLN includes libraries, library networks, archives, subject matter experts, online communities and library service providers. We believe every book ever published should be available as a high-quality print reproduction; printed on-demand anywhere in the world. This insures the ongoing accessibility of the content and helps generate sustainable revenue for the libraries and organizations that work to preserve these important materials.

The following book is in the "public domain" and represents an authentic reproduction of the text as printed by the original publisher. While we have attempted to accurately maintain the integrity of the original work, there are sometimes problems with the original work or the micro-film from which the books were digitized. This can result in minor errors in reproduction. Possible imperfections include missing and blurred pages, poor pictures, markings and other reproduction issues beyond our control. Because this work is culturally important, we have made it available as part of our commitment to protecting, preserving, and promoting the world's literature.

GUIDE TO FOLD-OUTS MAPS and OVERSIZED IMAGES

The book you are reading was digitized from microfilm captured over the past thirty to forty years. Years after the creation of the original microfilm, the book was converted to digital files and made available in an online database.

In an online database, page images do not need to conform to the size restrictions found in a printed book. When converting these images back into a printed bound book, the page sizes are standardized in ways that maintain the detail of the original. For large images, such as fold-out maps, the original page image is split into two or more pages

Guidelines used to determine how to split the page image follows:

• Some images are split vertically; large images require vertical and horizontal splits.
• For horizontal splits, the content is split left to right.
• For vertical splits, the content is split from top to bottom.
• For both vertical and horizontal splits, the image is processed from top left to bottom right.

DISSUASIVE

FROM

POPERY.

In a LETTER from the late Archbishop TILLOTSON, when Dean of *Canterbury*, to the Right Hon. CHARLES, then Earl, afterwards Duke of *Shrewsbury*.

LONDON:

Printed for JOHN RIVINGTON, Bookseller to *The* SOCIETY *for promoting Christian Knowledge*, at the Bible and Crown (N° 62.) in St Paul's Church-yard.
M DCC LXVIII.

PREFACE.

*A*S it is well known that Archbishop Tillotson, when Dean of Canterbury, had the principal Hand in disengaging that noble Personage Charles, then Earl, but afterwards Duke of Shrewsbury, from the Profession of the Roman Catholic Religion, in which he had been educated; so, we presume, it may well be esteemed a real Benefit conferred on the Publick, to produce the Arguments which he urged on the Occasion, and which were happily attended with so good an Effect. This we have now the Pleasure of doing, from a Manuscript in his own Hand-Writing. The Letter consisted originally of three Parts, viz.

I. *The Necessity of inquiring into the Grounds of our Religion.*

II. *The Protestant and Roman Catholic Religions compared.*

III. *Of Transubstantiation.*

The

PREFACE.

The two firſt Heads are here publiſhed verbatim (and they were never publiſhed before) from the Author's Manuſcript Copy. The third he printed Himſelf, perhaps a little enlarged, with a View of checking the Progreſs of Popery, under the Title of A Diſcourſe againſt Tranſubſtantiation, which is inſerted in his Works.

If theſe Parts were united again, and reduced to their original Form, the Whole would then make a very uſeful Treatiſe againſt Popery, excellently calculated to ſecure our People from the " ſly Inſinuations, and cun-
" ning Craftineſs of thoſe who lie in wait
" to deceive them."

With this View we have printed theſe two Parts of the Letter, in ſuch a manner, as to afford the Proprietors of the third a fair and convenient Opportunity of annexing theirs, and thereby of compleating the Whole.

TO THE

RIGHT HONOURABLE

THE

Earl of SHREWSBURY.

MY LORD,

SINCE that pleased God to incline your Lordship to take into your serious Consideration the Business of Religion, which of all other doth most nearly concern you, both in order to your present Peace and future Happiness, I cannot but be very glad of the Opportunity of being any ways serviceable to your Lordship upon so good an Occasion.

And because your Lordship hath thought fit to make use of my Advice in this weighty Matter, I shall with all Faithfulness give you the best Assistance I can, and shall offer nothing to your Consideration, but what, upon a free Examination of both Religions, I do most firmly believe myself.

That

That your Lordſhip determined not to make a Change before you are throughly convinced, is a very pious and wiſe Reſolution; but then ſurely this ought not to hinder your Lordſhip from proceeding to examine Things, in order to your full Satisfaction.

And whereas your Lordſhip is pleaſed to ſay, " that it is better to err on the believing Side than " the miſbelieving," I am verily perſuaded that God has not put Men under the hard neceſſity of erring dangerouſly on either Hand. However, this is a mere contingent Propoſition, which happens to be true or not, according as the Error we fall into, and the Conſequences of it are· but if it be taken for a certain Principle, and purſued as far as it will carry a Man, it may lead him into the greateſt Errors and Deluſions; becauſe by Virtue of it a Man ſhall be obliged, for fear of not believing ſo much as he ought, to believe whatever any Church or Religion hath either an Intereſt, or the Confidence to impoſe as an Article of Faith

I will trouble your Lordſhip no further but to recommend theſe Papers to your ſerious Peruſal; beſeeching the God of Truth ſo to diſpoſe and direct your Lordſhip's Mind in this great Enquiry, that you may clearly diſcern and ſincerely embrace the true Way to eternal Salvation. *I am,*

My LORD,

Your Lordſhip's moſt humble,

and moſt obedient Servant,

April 22, 1679.   JOHN TILLOTSON.

THAT your Lordship may proceed in this Matter with all the Care and Consideration that is due to so great a Concernment, I shall endeavour your Lordship's Satisfaction in this Method.

I. I shall vindicate the Reasonableness of Mens examining their Religion, and trying the Grounds of it whether they be firm or not.

II. I shall apply this to the Case under debate; and examine whether the Protestant Religion, or that of the Church of *Rome*, be the true Faith and Doctrine of CHRIST.

III. I shall particularly consider the Doctrine of *Transubstantiation*, not only because it is one of the most fundamental Articles of the Roman Religion, but because I perceive your Lordship is more particularly desirous to be clearly and fully satisfied in this Point.

Concerning the reasonableness of Mens examining their Religion, and the Grounds of it.

I. I shall endeavour to vindicate the reasonableness of Mens examining their Religion, and trying the Grounds of it, whether they be firm or not.

And for our clearer proceeding in this Matter, I must premise this Caution, that this is not a Duty equally and indifferently incumbent upon all; nor indeed fit and proper for all Persons, because all are not capable of it. There are two sorts of Persons that are either wholly, or in a great measure, incapable of it.

Children, and grown Persons of a very mean and low Capacity of Understanding —Children are not fit to examine, but only to learn and believe what is taught them by their Parents and Instructors.— And grown Persons, of a very low and mean Capacity of Understanding, and who either by reason of the Weakness of their Faculties, or other Disadvantages they lie under, are in little Probability of improving themselves· These are always to be looked upon as in the Condition of Children and Learners, and they must of necessity, in Things which are not plain and obvious to all Mankind, trust and rely upon the Judgement of others   And it is much safer and wiser for them so to do, than to lean to their own Understanding and depend upon their own Judgments.

And such Persons, if they be modest and humble, and pray to God for his Direction and Assistance, and are careful to practise what they know, and to live up to the best Light and Knowledge that they have, shall not miscarry only for Want of Knowledge, because their Ignorance is unavoidable, and God will require of them no more than he hath given, nor will call them to Account for those Talents which were never committed to them.   And if they be led into any dangerous Error by those under whose Care the Providence of God did put them, God will not impute it to them, because they took the best and wisest Course they could, to come to the Knowledge of the Truth.

But for those who by the Maturity of their Age, and by the natural Strength and Clearness of their Understandings, or by the Exercise and Improvement of them, are capable of enquiring into and understanding the Grounds of their Religion, and

discerning

diſcerning the Difference between Truth and Error, (I do not mean in nicer Points and of deeper Speculation, but in Matters of greater Moment and Importance in Religion,) it is very reaſonable that ſuch Perſons ſhould examine their Religion and the Grounds of it

And this muſt either be granted to be reaſonable, or elſe every Man muſt continue in that Religion in which he happens to be firſt by Education, or for any other Reaſon to pitch upon when he comes to Years, and firſt makes his Choice. For if this be a good Principle, that no Man is to examine his Religion, but to take it as it is, and to believe it, and reſt ſatisfied with it; then every Man is to remain in the Religion he firſt lights upon, whether by Choice or the Chance of his Education For he ought not to change but upon Reaſon; and Reaſon he can have none, unleſs he be allowed to examine his Religion, and to compare it with others, to ſee which is beſt, and ought in Reaſon to be choſen by him For to him that will not ſearch into the Reaſons and Grounds of any Religion, all Religions are alike, as all things are of the ſame Colour to him that lives always in the Dark; or if he be in the Light, will not open his Eyes, and uſe them to diſcern the different Colours of Things. But this is evidently unreaſonable at firſt Sight. For at this rate every Man that hath once embraced an Error, and a falſe Religion, muſt for ever continue in it, becauſe if he be not allowed to examine it, he can never have Reaſon to change and to make a Change without Reaſon, is unreaſonable, and mere Levity and Inconſtancy.

And yet, for all I can ſee, this is the Principle which the Church of *Rome* inculcates with great Zeal and Earneſtneſs upon their People, diſcouraging all Doubts about their Religion, as the Temptation of the Devil, and all Enquiry into the Grounds and

Reasons of it, as an Inclination to Herefy. What else do they mean by taking the Scriptures out of the Hands of the People, and locking them up from them in an unknown Tongue; by requiring them absolutely to submit their Judgments, and resign them up to the Crurch, and to believe as she believes, though they know not what that is ? That is, to believe as their Priest tells them : for that is all the teaching Part of the Church that the common People are acquainted with   And it is not sufficient to say, that when Men are in the Truth, and of the right Religion, and in the Bosom of the true Church, they ought to examine and enquire no further. This is manifestly unreasonable upon three Accounts.

1*st*, Because this is a plain begging of the Thing in Question, and that which every Church and every Religion does with equal Confidence pretend to—tnat theirs is the only true Church. And thefe Pretences are all alike reasonable, till the Grounds of them be examined, and compared together. And therefore it is the vaineft thing in the world for the Church of *Rome* to say, that all Religions in the world ought to be examined but their own ; because theirs and none else is the true Religion   For this which they say so confidently of it, that it is the true Religion, no Man can know till he hath examined it, and searched into the Grounds of it, and considered the Objections that are against it. So that it is fond Partiality to say, that their Religion is not to be examined by the People which profess it, but all others ought to be examined. Because every Religion and every Church may (for ought appears to any Man that is not suffered to examine) say the same for themselves, and with as much Reason. And if so, then either every Religion ought to permit itself to be examined,

amined, or no Man ought to examine his own Religion, whatever it be   And consequently Jews, and *Turks*, and Heathens, and Hereticks, ought all to continue as they are, and none of them to change; because they cannot reasonably change without examining both that Religion which they leave, and that which they embrace instead of it.

2*dly*, Admitting this Pretence were true, that they are the true Church, and have the true Religion; this is so far from being a Reason why they should not permit it to be examined, that, on the contrary, it is one of the best Reasons in the world both why they should permit it to be examined, and why they may safely suffer it to be so.

They should permit it to be tried, that Men may upon good Reason be satisfied that it is the true Religion. And they may safely do it, because if they be sure that the Grounds of their Religion be firm and good, I am sure they will be never the worse for being examined and looked into.   But I appeal to every Man, whether it be not a shrewd Sign that they are not sure that the Grounds of their Religion are sound and firm, and such as will abide the trial, that they are so loth to have them examined and looked into ? This would tempt a wise Man to suspect they know something that is amiss in their Religion, which makes them so loth to have it narrowly searched into and examined.

3*dly*, It is certain among all Christians, that the Doctrine preached by the Apostles was the true Faith of CHRIST; and yet they never forbad Christians to examine whether it were so or not: nay, on the contrary, they exhorted every one to try and examine their Religion, and whether that Doctrine which they had
delivered

delivered to them was the true Faith of CHRIST. So St *Paul*, 2 Cor. xiii 5. *Examine yourselves, whether ye be in the Faith; Prove your ounselves* And again, 1 *Thess* v 21. *Prove all things; hold fast that which is good* And so likewise St *John*, 1 Epist. iv. 1. *Beloved, believe not every Spirit, but try the Spirits whether they be of God Because many false Prophets are gone out into the World.* And St *Luke*, *Acts* xvii. 11. commends it as a noble and generous Quality in the *Bereans*, because they examined the Doctrine which the Apostles preached, to see whether it were agreeable to the Scriptures · *These*, says he, *were more noble than those in Theffalonica, in that they received the Word with all readiness of Mind, and searched the Scriptures daily, whether those things were so.*

We desire no more of the Church of *Rome*, but that they encourage their People to search the Scriptures daily, and to examine whether their Doctrines be according to them. I would fain hear a Pope commend to the People the searching of the Scriptures to try their Doctrines by it, and praise them for doing it.

But it is a great while since the Pope hath declared his dislike of this generous Disposition in the People, of searching the Scriptures

A mean and servile Spirit, that will trust him and the Church without ever desiring to look into the Bible, is far more acceptable to him, and will serve his turn much better.

You see then. upon the whole matter, that it is a groundless and suspicious Pretence of the Church of *Rome*, that because they are infallibly in the right, and theirs the true Religion, therefore their People ought not to be permitted to examine it.

The Doctrine of the Apostles was undoubtedly the true Faith of CHRIST; and yet they not only permitted

ted the People to examine it, but exhorted and encouraged them so to do, and commended them for it. And any Man that hath the Spirit of a Man, would abhor to submit to this Slavery, and break with the Pope upon this single Point, and tell him plainly, " If your Religion be too good to be examined, I " doubt it is too bad to be believed."

If it be said, that the allowing of this Liberty is the Way to make People perpetually doubting and unsettled.—I utterly deny this, and affirm, that it is apt to have the contrary Effect. there being no better Way in the world to establish any Man in the Belief of Religion, than to let him see that there are very good Grounds and Reasons for what he believes; which no Man can see, that is not permitted to examine whether they be so or not.

The Proteſtant Religion and that of the Church of *Rome* compared.

I Come now to apply the former Diſcourſe to the Caſe under debate; and examine whether the Proteſtant Religion, or that of the Church of *Rome*, be the true Faith and Doctrine of CHRIST.

And this will beſt appear by comparing them together; in which compariſon I will inſiſt upon three Things which will bring this Trial to an Iſſue, and are ſufficient to determine every ſober and conſiderate Man, which of theſe Religions he ought in Reaſon, and with Regard to the Safety of his own Soul, to embrace

And

And they are thefe

1*ft*, That the Proteftants govern their Belief and Practice in Matters of Religion by the true ancient Rule of Chriftianity—the Word of GOD, contained in the holy Scriptures: But the Papifts, for the maintaining of their Errors and Corruptions, have been forced to devife a rew Rule, never owned by the primitive Church, nor by the ancient Councils and Fathers cf it.

2*dly*, That the Doctrines and Practices in Difference between us and the Church of *Rome*, are either contrary to this Rule, or deftitute of the Warrant and Authority of it—and plain Additions to the ancient Chriftianity, and Corruptions of it.

3*dly*, That the Proteftant Religion hath many clear Advantages of Popery, very confiderable in themfelves, and difcernible to every Eye upon the very Propofal of them.

1*ft*, That the Proteftants govern their Belief and Practice in Matters of Religion by the true ancient Rule of Chriftianity—the Word of GOD, contained in the holy Scriptures: But the Papifts, for the maintaining of their Errors and Corruptions, have been forced to devife a new Rule, never owned by the primitive Church, nor by the ancient Councils and Fathers of it: That is, they have joined with the Word of GOD, contained in the holy Scriptures, the unwritten Traditions of their Church, concerning feveral Points of Faith and Practice, which they acknowledge cannot be proved from the Scriptures. And thefe they call the unwritten Word of GOD,

which

which the Council of *Trent* hath declared to be of equal Authority with the holy Scriptures, and to be recieved and believed with the same pious Affection and Reverence; contrary to the express Declaration and unanimous Consent of all the ancient Councils and Fathers of the christian Church; and never declared to be a Point of Faith, until it was decreed (not much above an hundred Years ago) in the Council of *Trent*. And this is surely, if any Thing is, a Matter of great Consequence, to presume to alter the ancient Rule of the Christian Doctrine, and to add to it at their Pleasure. But the Church of *Rome* having changed the Doctrine of Christianity, it became necessary to them to change the Rule of it too. And therefore with great Reason did the Council of *Trent* take this into Consideration in the first Place, and place it in the Front of their Decrees; because it was so necessary to make good a great Part of those which followed

2*dly*, I shall endeavour to shew, that the Doctrines and Practices in Difference between us and the Church of *Rome*, are either contrary to the true ancient Rule of Christianity, or destitute of the Warrant and Authority of it, ——and plain Additions to the ancient Christianity, or Corruptions of it The Truth of this will best appear, by instancing in the principal Doctrines and Practices in Difference between us

As for their two great fundamental Doctrines, of the Supremacy of the Bishop of *Rome* over all the Christians in the World, and his Infallibility; there is not one Word in Scripture concerning either of these Privileges conferred upon him

Nay, it is little less than Demonstration, that they had no such Privileges, that St *Paul*, in his long Epistle to the Church of *Rome*, takes no Notice either

ther

ther of the Supremacy or Infallibility of their Bishop; or of that Church being the Mother and Mistress of all Churches. which is now an Article of Faith in the Church of *Rome*. And it is hardly possible to imagine, that he could have omitted to take Notice of such remarkable Privileges of their Bishop and Church above any in the World, had he known they belonged to them   He was certainly ignorant of these mighty Prerogatives of the Church of *Rome*, otherways it cannot be but that he would have written with more Deference and Submission to this Seat of Infallibility, and Center of Unity.   He would certainly have paid a greater Respect to this Mother and Mistress of all Churches, where the Head of the Church, and the Vicar of CHRIST, was designed for ever to fix his Throne, and establish his Residence. But there is not one word, nor the least intimation of any such thing, throughout his whole Epistle.

Besides that both these pretended Privileges are confuted by plain Fact, and the Evidence of Things themselves. —— Their Supremacy ; in that the far greatest Part of the Christian Church neither is at this Day, nor can be shewn by the Records of any Age, ever to have been subject to the Bishop of *Rome*, or to have acknowledged his Authority and Jurisdiction over them.—And the Infallibility of the Pope, whether with or without a General Council (about which they are not yet agreed, though Infallibility was invented on purpose to determine all Differences) I say, this Infallibility, wherever it is, is plainly confuted by the contradictory Decrees of several Popes and Councils   And if they have contradicted one another, there must be an Error on one side.

Their Service in an unknown Tongue ;

Their forbidding the People the Use of the Scriptures ,

Their

Their Communion in one Kind,

Their Worship of Images ;

Their Invocations of Angels, of the blessed Virgin, and of Saints, in the same solemn manner, and for the same Things that we pray to GOD himself for; are all Practices which we are able to prove to be plainly contrary to the Word of GOD; and, as the learned of their own Church acknowledge, there is neither Precept nor Example for them there; nor were they practised by the Christian Church for several Ages. And this Acknowledgement we think to be a mighty Advantage, considering how great a Part of their Religion, especially as practised among the common People, is contained in these five Points.

For the Service of GOD in an unknown Tongue, and withholding the Scriptures from the People, they do not pretend so much as one Testimony of any Father for above six hundred Years. And nothing in the world was ever more unreasonable, especially considering, that they will not allow any to be saved out of their Church; and yet they deny Men the most necessary and effectual Means of Salvation when they are in it, the Knowledge of the Scriptures, and the Understanding of their Prayers. And is not this a very hard Case, when, in Effect, they will neither let Men be saved in their Church, nor out of it?

The two great *Doctrines* of *Transubstantiation* and *Purgatory*, are acknowledged by very many of their most learned Writers to have no certain Foundation in Scripture, and I am sure they can have none any where else.

That there are Seven Sacraments of the Christian Religion, though it be now made an Article of Faith by the Council of *Trent* is a Thing which cannot be shewn to have been affirmed by any Council or Father for above a thousand Years after CHRIST; and

perhaps

perhaps was first said by *Peter Lombard*, the Father of the Schoolmen, and long since his time hath been made a matter necessary to Salvation to be believed, or at least damnable to be denied

That the Church of *Rome* is the Mother and Mistress of all Churches, though that also be one of the new Articles of Pope *Pius* IV his Creed, which all Priests are by a solemn Oath obliged to believe and teach, yet is most evidently false That she is not the Mother of all Churches is plain, because *Jerusalem* was certainly so · for there was the first Christian Church, and from thence all the Churches in the world derived themselves And that she is not, though she fair would be, the Mistress of all Churches, is as evident, because the greatest Part of the Christian Church does at this Day, and always did deny that she had any Authority or Supremacy over them.

Now these are the principal Matters in Difference between us, and if these Points, and a few more, be pared off from Popery, that which remains of their Religion is the same with ours ; that is, the true ancient Christianity

3*dly*, I shall shew, that the Protestant Religion hath many Advantages of Popery, considerable in themselves and discernible to every Eye upon the very Proposal of them

1*st*, That our Religion agrees with the Scriptures, and all Points both of our Belief and Practice, esteemed by us necessary to Salvation, are confessedly there contained, our Enemies themselves being Judges.

We " worship the Lord our God, and him only do we serve " We do not fall down before Images, and worship them

We address our Prayers to God alone, by the only Mediation and Intercession of his Son Jesus Christ, as St *Paul* directs us, giving us this very good Reason for it, *Becauf there is but one God, and one Mediator between God and Man, the Man Chrift Jefus.*

The publick Service of God, is performed by us in a known Tongue, according to St *Paul's* exprefs Order and Direction, and the univerfal Practice of the ancient Church, and the Reafon of the Thing itfelf.

We adminifter the Sacrament of the Lord's Sup. in both Kinds, according to our Saviour's Example and plain Precept and Inftitution, and the continual Practice of all the Chriftian Churches in the world for above a thoufand Years.

2*dly*, We believe nothing as neceffary to Salvation but what hath been owned in all Ages to be Chriftian Doctrine, and is fo acknowledged to be by the Church of *Rome* itfelf.

And we receive the whole Faith of the primitive Church, viz whatever is contained in the Apoftles Creed, and the Creeds of the four firft General Councils

By which it evidently appears, that all Points of Faith in Difference between us and the Church of *Rome*, are plain Additions to the ancient Chriftian Faith.

3*dly*, There is nothing wanting in our Church and Religion, either in Matter of Faith or Practice, which either the Scripture makes neceffary to Salvation, or was fo efteemed by the Chriftian Church for the firft five hundred Years. And we truft that what was fufficient for the Salvation of Chriftians in the beft Ages of Chriftianity for five hundred Years together, may be fo ftill

4*thly*, Our Religion is not only free from Idolatry, but from all Sufpicion and probable Charge of it, which the Church of *Rome* is not as is acknowledged

ed by her moſt learned Champions, and no Man of
Ingenuity can deny.

5*thly*. Our Religion is not encumbered with ſu-
perſtitious and troubleſome, and ridiculous Obſer-
vances, as theirs infinitely is, even beyond the Ce-
remonial Law of *Moſes*, to the great Burden and
Scandal of Religion, and the diverting of Mens
Minds from the ſpiritual Part of it, and the more
weighty and neceſſary Duties of the Chriſtian Life.
So that in truth a devout Papiſt is ſo taken up with
the external Rites and little Tricks of his Religion,
that he hath no time to be a good Man, and to cul-
tivate his Mind in true Piety and Virtue.

6*thly*. Our Religion is evidently more charitable
to all Chriſtians that differ from us And of all things
in the world, methinks, the want of Charity in any
Church ſhould be a Motive to no Man to be in love
with it, and fond of its Communion

7*thly*, Our Religion does not claſh and interfere
with any of the great moral Duties, to which all Man
kind ſtand obliged by the Law and Light of Nature,
as Fidelity, Mercy, and Truth We do not teach
Men to break Faith with Hereticks, or to extirpate
thoſe who differ from us with Fire and Sword, by
an Inquiſition, or a Maſſacre No ſuch thing as
Equivocation, and mental Reſervation, or any other
artificial Way of Lying is either taught or juſtified,
either by the Doctrine, or the Caſuiſts of our Church.
But I know a certain famous Church in the World,
in which all theſe Things, ſo odious even to the
Light of Nature, are not only frequently practiſed,
but publickly taught, and avowed and maintained
to be lawful

8*thly*, Our Religion is perfectly conſiſtent with
civil Government, and neither exempts the Clergy
from Subjection to the civil Power, nor abſolves
Subjects

Subjects, upon any Pretence whatsoever, from their Allegiance to their Prince,——— both which Points are stiffly maintained by the Church of *Rome* as necessary to Salvation

9*thly*, The Doctrines of our Religion are perfectly free from all Suspicion of worldly Interest and Design Whereas the Pope's Kingdom is plainly of this World; and his Doctrines are of this World, and are ready upon all Occasions, like so many Servants, to fight for him. For most of them do plainly tend either to the Encouragement of his Authority, and the Establishment of his Tyranny over the Church, as the Doctrines of Supremacy and Infallibility; or to the magnifying of the Priests, and giving them a perfect Power over the Consciences of the People, and keeping them in a slavish Subjection and blind Obedience to them. And to these Purposes tend the Doctrines of exempting the Clergy from the secular Power.———Of *Transubstantiation,* which must needs make the Priest a great Man in the Opinion of the People, because he can make GOD: and this Doctrine being once swallowed, they may thrust down any thing after it.———The Communicating of the Laity only in one Kind, it being the sole Privilege of the Priests to receive in both.———The withholding of the Scriptures from the People, and the Service in an unknown Tongue.———The Doctrine of an implicit Faith, and an absolute Resignation of their Judgements to their Teachers, to keep the People in Ignorance, and bring them to a blind Obedience to their Dictates.———The Necessity of the Intention of the Priest, to the saving Virtue and Efficacy of the the Sacraments; by which Doctrine, the People do in a manner depend as much upon the good Will of the Priest as upon the Mercy of GOD for their Salvation.———And above all, that of the absolute

Necessity

Necessity of private Confession of all their Sins to the Priest, not only for the Direction of their Consciences, but as a necessary Condition of the Pardon and Forgiveness of their Sins By which Device they make themselves Masters of all the Secrets of the People, and keep them in Awe by the Knowledge of their Faults *Scire volunt secreta Domus atque inde timeri.*———Or else their Doctrines tend to filthy Lucre, and the enriching of the Church; as the Doctrine of *Purgatory*, and Indulgences, and Prayers and Masses for the Dead, and many more of the like Kind.

10*thly*, Our Religion is free from all dishonest Arts of maintaining and supporting itself. Such are their clipping of Authors, even those of their own Church, when they speak too freely of any Points, by an *Index Expurgatorius* ; and those three gross and shameful Forgeries of the Church of *Rome*,—1. Of the Canon of the Council of *Nice*, in the Case of Appeals between *Rome* and the *African* Church ;—2 *Constantine*'s Donation to the Popes ;— 3. And the Decretal Epistles of the Ancient Popes, a large Volume of Forgeries compiled by *Isidore Mercator*, to countenance the Popes Usurpations , of which the Church of *Rome* made use for several Ages, and pertinaciously defended the Authority of them, till the learned Men of their own Church have at last been forced, for very Shame, to disclaim them, and to confess the Imposture of them. A like Instance to which I shall challenge any Man to shew among the Protestants. This is playing with false Dice when the eternal Salvation of Mens Souls lies at Stake

Lastly, That I may bring back this Discourse to my former: Our Religion hath this mighty Advantage, that it doth not decline Trial and Examination;
which

which to any Man of Ingenuity muft needs appear very fair and honeft But if any Church refufe to have her Religion examined, and her Doctrines brought into Light, it is plain Evidence that fhe hath fome Diftruft of them There needs no more to render their Religion fufpected to a wife Man, than that they are fo fhy and fearful it fhould be looked into; and that the People fhould know what can be faid againft it And this is too vifible in the Methods which they commonly ufe of feducing Men to their Religion; much like thofe which Cheats practife upon a young Heir, when they have infinuated themfelves into his Company and good Opinion :—They charge him not to tell his Friends what Company he hath been in, to afk no body's Advice, to hearken to no Counfel contrary to what they perfuade him.

Juft thus the Factors and Emiffaries of the Church of *Rome* practife upon weak People. They charge them not to acquaint their Minifter with what they have faid to them; to read no Books to the contrary, becaufe they are no Judges of Points of Faith · and yet if they be not, why do they offer Arguments to perfuade them to be of their Religion? Thefe are fuch grofs and infincere Ways of proceeding, that tney betray themfelves, and plainly difcover thofe that make ufe of them to have no fair and honeft Defign. And methinks, of the two, a Man of Under-ftanding and Confcience fhould hate and fcorn more to be rooked out of his Religion, than out of his Ef-tate.

I might have infifted largely upon each of thefe Particulars: any one of whch is fufficient to incline a Man ftrongly to the Proteftant, Religion and to fet his Heart againft Popery: But all of them toge-ther make fo powerful an Argument to an unpreju-
diced

diced Person, as does almost irresistably determine his Choice. They are so plain at first hearing, that they cannot be denied to be clear Advantages of our Religion over that of the Church of *Rome*

III. A Discourse on Transubstantiation.

This is printed in a separate Tract, and may be had of J. RIVINGTON. *Price 3d.* or 20*s*. a Hundr.

Lightning Source UK Ltd.
Milton Keynes UK
UKHW031836010421
381387UK00006B/55